THE SOWER
and His Bible

Magnify the Word Series
Evangelist Paul Schwanke

Evangelist Paul Schwanke
www.preachthebible.com

Special thanks to Miss Kelly Schwanke
Special thanks to Cathy

ISBN-13: 978-1725803947
ISBN-10: 1725803941

Printed in the United States of America

CONTENTS

Magnify the Word

FROM WITHOUT and from within, the Bible is under assault. While it is expected that Satan and his forces will use our pagan culture to attack the precious Word of God, the more alarming trend is the erosion of passion for the Bible in the hearts and lives of God's people. Despite the multitude of verses which constantly command us to keep and guard the Scriptures, far too many people seem content to abandon the Word of God in favor of new ideas and thinking. Of course, these 'fresh' perspectives are nothing but a rebranding of Satan's first recorded words: *"Yea, hath God said."*

To the liberal seminary professors, the Bible is a good book; even a great book, but nothing more. They may concede that the Bible 'contains' the Word of God, but they as 'experts' are needed so that the common man can understand which parts of the Bible do and do not apply in our present day.

To the modern minister, the Bible is an authority, but not the only authority. Personal encounters and experiences, dreams and visions, and human thoughts and ideas can be as inspired as the Bible.

The Fundamentalist would boldly say that the Bible is the 'final authority.' The problem, of course, is that this thinking allows for multiple authorities. While it is true these other authorities are not as important as the Bible, these preachers, theologians, fellowship leaders, and professors are set up as human authorities on matters of belief.

Since the first century, Independent Baptist people have been recognized as those who believe that the Bible is the only rule of faith and practice. It is not an authority; it is not an important authority; it is not the supreme authority; it is the **only** authority. The *Magnify the Word Series* is a collection of books written to encourage the saints of God to return to their first love for the Book.

"I will worship toward thy holy temple,
and praise thy name
for thy lovingkindness and for thy truth:
for thou hast magnified thy word
above all thy name."
(Psalm 138:2)

Luke 8:4-15

And when much people were gathered together, and were come to him out of every city, he spake by a parable: A sower went out to sow his seed: and as he sowed, some fell by the way side; and it was trodden down, and the fowls of the air devoured it. And some fell upon a rock; and as soon as it was sprung up, it withered away, because it lacked moisture. And some fell among thorns; and the thorns sprang up with it, and choked it. And other fell on good ground, and sprang up, and bare fruit an hundredfold. And when he had said these things, he cried, He that hath ears to hear, let him hear. And his disciples asked him, saying, What might this parable be? And he said, Unto you it is given to know the mysteries of the kingdom of God: but to others in parables; that seeing they might not see, and hearing they might not understand. Now the parable is this: The seed is the word of God. Those by the way side are they that hear; then cometh the devil, and taketh away the word out of their hearts, lest they should believe and be saved. They on the rock are they, which, when they hear, receive the word with joy; and these have no root, which for a while believe, and in time of temptation fall away. And that which fell among thorns are they, which, when they have heard, go forth, and are choked with cares and riches and pleasures of this life, and bring no fruit to perfection. But that on the good ground are they, which in an honest and good heart, having heard the word, keep it, and bring forth fruit with patience.

Introduction

THE CROWDS ARE MASSIVE. Terms like "great multitudes," "great company," "whole multitude," and "much people" describe the throngs that come to see Jesus. His "fame" spreads from the Galilee region throughout the entire country. They come to Him from the north, south, east, and west.

The crowds won't let Him go. They 'press' Him to hear the preaching. They pack out the house where He is teaching, and the only way to get the lame man to Him is by cutting a hole in the roof. For the ministers who count the numbers to determine success, this is the apex. Big crowds mean it must be right.[1]

So what will Jesus do now? The mega church ministers would no doubt advise Him as to the next step. "Listen to our great 'ideas.' You must give them music that they like. You need to bring in celebrities and politicians to make the crowd grow. You need to have a party atmosphere - let's call it a celebration - no let's call it a 'festival.' You need to give them an 'entry-level church' experience!"

But instead, Jesus does the unthinkable. He does precisely what the Madison Avenue advertising experts tell us not to do. He violates the Rick Warren rules on how to grow a church.[2]

He confuses them.

I remember sitting in Sunday School as a child and hearing this: "Parables are earthly stories that picture heavenly truths." Jesus has a different definition. He said, "Unto you it is given to know the mysteries of the kingdom of God: but to others in parables; that seeing they might not see, and hearing they might not understand" (Luke 8:10). Though it is true the parables rise from the stories of everyday life, the interpretation, by design, bewilders most listeners.

One might read those words and conclude that Jesus did not want the people to understand what He was teaching. Such a conclusion is correct. Although this thinking is unfathomable in our modern era, as religion does its best to dumb down the Bible, it is precisely what Jesus is teaching.

The parables are not for everyone!

Jesus uses the parables not only to build the faith of those who trust Him, but they are also used to judge those who reject Him. The parables are part of His winnowing process. His children will get it, but those who don't will actually be worse for hearing. Seven and a half centuries earlier, the prophet Isaiah put it in no uncertain terms:

"And he said, Go, and tell this people, Hear ye indeed, but understand not; and see ye indeed, but perceive not. Make the heart of this people fat, and make their ears heavy, and shut their eyes; lest they see with their eyes, and hear with their ears, and understand with their heart, and convert, and be healed" (Isaiah 6:9-10).

As Jesus makes His way through the highways and byways of Israel, the first century crowd identifies Him in a myriad of ways. Perhaps the finest testimony comes from the mouth of Peter: "Thou art the Christ, the Son of the living God" (Matthew 16:16). Perhaps the most wicked comes from the nameless crowd: "He hath a devil, and is mad; why hear ye him" (John 10:20)? From bowing at His feet to putting Him on the Cross, the people then, like most people today, have strong views of Jesus.

To make things more confusing, Satan always has plenty of substitute messiahs ready to do his bidding. The warnings ring from the pages of the Bible: "Even now are there many antichrists; whereby we know that it is the last time" (1 John 2:18). "Many deceivers are entered into the world, who confess not that Jesus Christ is come in the flesh. This is a deceiver and an antichrist" (2 John 7). In such a confusing environment, Jesus bursts on the scene. How are the people to know that He is the true Christ?

The answer is found in John 5:39: "Search the scriptures; for in them ye think ye have eternal life: *and they are they which testify of me.*" God never tells people to trust their feelings. God never tells people to follow a religion. He tells them to open the Bible and see what it says.

Students of the Bible know the Savior will be born in Bethlehem. Students of the Bible know that God will send the forerunner who will prepare the way. Students of the Bible know that Jesus will perform specific miracles to prove his claims. Students of the Bible know right where to find Him.

The miracles of Jesus are not simply random acts of kindness upon a people beloved of God, they are a trenchant testimony to the fact that Jesus is the Messiah. When John the Baptist is imprisoned, he sends his disciples to Jesus to find out if He is truly the Promised One. The answer of Jesus is significant: "Go and shew John again those things which ye do hear and see: The blind receive their sight, and the lame walk, the lepers are cleansed, and the deaf hear, the dead are raised up, and the poor have the gospel preached to them" (Matthew 11:4-5). Jesus is telling John to open his Bible to the book of Isaiah and see what God predicted about the Christ.

Jesus is the Son of God because the Bible says so! The Scriptures testify of Him!

The miracles of Christ have a greater purpose than a temporary healing or the fixing of a problem. The miracles, clearly prophesied in the Old Testament, are the means by which people will know that Jesus is the Son of God. Sadly, most of the humans who eat his food, revel in his teaching, and are the beneficiaries of His miracles, refuse to give Him praise and honor. "Were there not ten cleansed? but where *are* the nine" (Luke 17:17)? They take their gifts and go back to their old way of life.

The disciples of Jesus, which include men and women who are not part of the twelve apostles (Luke 8:3), are those who listened to John the Baptist. Now they are rejoicing in His mighty works, but even more, they are feasting on His teaching and preaching. These are the people for whom the nearly sixty parables in the New Testament are given.

"And when much people
were gathered together,
and were come to him out of every city,
he spake by a parable:
A sower went out to sow his seed..."

Chapter One

THE EXPERTS tell us this is the *Parable of the Sower*, but the Bible never uses that title. A far more appropriate name would be the *Parable of the Seed*, because the emphasis is not on the human sower, it is on the Word of God. In fact, the word 'sower' is found but one time in Luke 8. The attention is given to the Scriptures: *"The seed is the word of God."*

The lesson should not be missed. We need more of the Bible and less of the preacher. We need more of the Scriptures and less of the scholars. We need more of God's Word and less human opinion.

The scene is a common one in New Testament times. It is the rainy season between October and December. It is any day of the week except the Sabbath. The farmer carries a bag of grain over his shoulder. He reaches into the bag and tosses the seeds as he walks past the rows.[3] As someone living in the Midwest would readily recognize a farmer plowing the field, the people listening in Luke 8 have a vivid picture painted in their minds.

The sower tosses his seed with an eye towards the following June. He is hoping for a harvest. He will throw a lot of seed on the ground knowing that three quarters of the seed will not bear fruit.[4] He is very liberal in tossing the seed, because he never knows what will happen.

Jesus goes on to describe four scenarios. In the first, some of the seed "fell by the way side; and it was trodden down, and the fowls of the air devoured it." The "way side" is the path where the farmers walk to access their crops. In the dry, arid lands of the Mediterranean desert, such ground becomes too hard to plow. The seed that falls on these paths is an easy meal for the fowls of the air. They can't wait to "devour" it.

The second possibility allows for the seed to fall on a "rock." In the hill country of Galilee, a thin layer of dirt hides the great limestone beneath it. The picture is not so much of a field full of rocks, but rather one that appears to be a very promising place to plant seed. The discouragement sets in when the farmer discovers that the rocky layer below the surface will not allow the plants to receive moisture. Soon, the plant withers and dies.[5]

Next, Jesus says that "some fell among thorns; and the thorns sprang up with it, and choked it." These thorns grow like weeds in the region. They can grow to a height of six feet and bud with red, blue, or yellow flowers.[6] They may be impressive, they may be colorful, but in the end, they are destructive. They choke the good seed.

Finally, there are seeds that fall "on good ground." "By their fruits ye shall know them" (Matthew 7:20). Months later, the sower rejoices for the good seed has found root. There is not only a harvest, but there is also an abundant harvest. A return of thirty-five grains would be average, but an "hundredfold" harvest is exceptional! Such a return makes one forget about the seeds that fail.

Lessons abound for the sower who loves the Bible:

The Sower Sows with Purpose

"A sower went out to sow his seed." The reminder is simple, yet, must not be forgotten - the sower is on offense. He goes out to the harvest fields.

For Jesus, the harvest fields full of lost sinners matter more to Him than eating. He tells His disciples, "My meat is to do the will of him that sent me, and to finish his work. Say not ye, There are yet four months, and *then* cometh harvest? … Lift up your eyes, and look on the fields; for they are white already to harvest" (John 4:34-35).

I have seen missionary organizations that have massive support staff filling mission compounds, but no one is going forth with the Bible. Preachers can spend the day staring at a computer screen, but the lost world needs the seed of the Word of God. The Great Commission starts with the word "go." We have more than enough analysis; we need more obedience.

The Sower Sows Everywhere

The sower tosses the seed in every direction only to learn that most of the seed is wasted. He knows beforehand that the birds of the sky, the stone beneath him, and the weeds will do their best to steal the harvest. But he also knows that some of the seed will find root. The more seed that he tosses upon the ground, the greater his chances of a good crop.

What an encouragement for the preacher who sows the Word of God! What an encouragement for the soul-winner with a heart to see people saved! "So shall my word be that goeth forth out of my mouth: it shall not return unto me void, but it shall accomplish that which I please, and it shall prosper *in the thing* whereto I sent it" (Isaiah 55:11). Because it is impossible to look at human faces and know the condition of the heart, the wise sower will 'toss' as much Bible as he can. He never knows what verse will penetrate the sinful heart, but he is confident that God's words will produce God's results.

Monroe Parker was a mighty preacher of the last century. For more than sixty years, he traveled the world faithfully balancing solid Bible preaching with an earnest passion for souls. He was one of the last evangelists of an era when such God-called men were seeing mighty results.

As a young preacher, I had the privilege of enjoying a meal with him. He was incredibly gracious and helpful in dispensing advice and wisdom. As we were going our separate ways, his last words to me are the ones that I best remember: "Brother, give 'em the Bible!"

Keep preaching the word "in season...out of season" (2 Timothy 4:2). "And let us not be weary in well doing: for in due season we shall reap, if we faint not" (Galatians 6:9). "Therefore seeing we have this ministry, as we have received mercy, we faint not" (2 Corinthians 4:1).

"Give 'em the Bible!"

The Sower Does Not Know Which Seed Will Bring a Harvest

One of the great lessons a sower learns is the importance of trusting the Word. There is a reason God's man is to "declare ... all the counsel of God" (Acts 20:27). It is all too common for the sower to think he needs to create a captivating message that will impress the hearer. We think our smooth words, our polished message, or our brilliant logic is the crying need of the sinner.

But the Bible sower learns that the Holy Spirit is more than able to use the Scripture in ways he never imagined. God's Words are the effective words. The power of the Word of God in conjunction with the power of the Spirit of God is able to go into the smallest crevices of the human hearts and accomplish what He pleases. This is the reason we cannot pick and choose which parts of the Bible we will use, and which parts we will ignore.

As the sower reaches into the bag and grabs the seed, he has no idea which seed will work. As the Bible preacher opens the Scriptures and preaches the Word, he has no idea which verse will influence a life. As the personal witness for Christ testifies of the Savior, he has no idea what is happening in the heart of his friend. The best advice is found in Psalm 126:6:

"He that goeth forth and weepeth,
bearing precious seed,
shall doubtless come again with rejoicing,
bringing his sheaves with him."

The Sower Does Not Always Know What the Ground is Like

When the seed falls on the rock, it begins to germinate. For a while, it is 'so far; so good.' Time reveals the hardness below.

Every sower understands this point. We have all had our own early harvests that did not pan out as we expected. We have also seen harvest where we thought it was impossible for seed to grow. When the Lord told Ezekiel, "neither be dismayed at their looks" (Ezekiel 3:9), He was dispensing advice for the ages. We simply cannot tell from the look on a face what is happening in the heart.

The Sower Must be Patient

The seeds that fell on the good ground ultimately "sprang up" and "bare fruit." For months, the sower doesn't know what is going to happen. He invests his time, his energy, and his money into a venture that has no guarantees. Many variables that are out of his control will contribute to the final result. He must look to Heaven, because he knows that he cannot send the rain nor provide the sunshine.

Yet, the sower keeps on sowing. We cannot be weary in the work. Harvest comes in "due season." We are tempted to look at human success stories and see large ministries and massive buildings, but God notices the preacher who spends decades with the same people. God notices the bus worker who gives up his Saturday mornings laboring among neglected people. God notices the Sunday School teacher who invests his life in boys and girls. "Moreover it is required in stewards, that a man be found faithful" (1 Corinthians 4:2).

A survey made by the National Retail Dry Goods Association reveals the following results:

- 48% of the salesmen make one call and quit
- 25% make two calls and quit
- 15% make three calls and quit

But 12% keep on calling. They do 80% of the business. The 88% who quit after the first, second, or third calls do only 20% of the business.[7]

God has called us to be sowers. It is not just the man behind the pulpit, every child of God has a responsibility. "He that goeth forth and weepeth, bearing precious seed, shall doubtless come again with rejoicing, bringing his sheaves *with him"* (Psalm 126:6).

Let's "give 'em the Bible." And when we have done that, let's "give 'em the Bible" again. It is how the sower does the work.

Chapter Two

"AND WHEN HE had said these things, he cried, He that hath ears to hear, let him hear." When Jesus walks on this earth, He speaks these words on seven different occasions.[8] After His resurrection, He uses the same phrase eight more times.[9] John Phillips points out: "The first use of the expression warns us against careless hearing of the Word of God. The final use warns against worshiping the Antichrist. The one instance shows where unbelief begins; the other instance shows where it ends."[10]

It is the invitation that Jesus gives to the listeners. "Much people" hear Him deliver the 'Parable of the Seed,' but they do not get it. Though they all have human ears that hear Him speak the words, they do not have spiritual ears to comprehend them. It is interesting to note that Jesus 'speaks' the parable, but he 'cries' the invitation. 'Leading the horse to the water' and 'getting him to drink' are certainly two different things.

The men and ladies following Him ask, "What might this parable be?" This simple questions separates the crowd from the disciples. The people come to get something from Him; the disciples come to learn from Him. "Learn of me" (Matthew 11:24) is the command of Jesus they take to heart. At the end of the day, many people can say that they had heard Him speak. Not many, however, can say they had learned of Him.

118 million Americans will visit a house of religion next Sunday morning wanting something from Jesus. Some are looking for entertainment, some are looking for encouragement, some are looking for healing, some are looking for prosperity, but most are like the multitudes of Luke 8. They will hear a few words and walk away satisfied. These houses of religion will not be open on Sunday night because these people don't want any more. On Monday morning, they will tell their friends they went to church, they will feel good

about their experience, but their lives will not be changed.

To the few who want to know more about Jesus, the Savior explains the parable. These are the ones who will know, see, and understand. The point should be clear. The truth of the Bible is available to all of us, but we are going to have to ask. He will never force His word down our throats.

As Jesus explains the various soils that receive the Word, He describes the human hearts that hear the Word of God. We are taught what to expect as we preach the Word. We are taught how to expect people to respond as we witness to them. Every human heart is different.

Some Soil is Hardened Soil

Jesus compares the hardened way side to hard hearts. These hearts have no desire for the Bible. They have been battered over the years by sin and its cumulative influence. The seed hits and bounces off. Such a heart is easy prey for Satan and his forces.

The "way side" does not harden overnight. Through the course of time, people walk on the way side, rain pummels the way side, and the ground cannot be plowed. Many attendees on a Sunday morning have gradually hardened themselves to God's Word. They may sit in a service by order of mom and dad, they may attend to please a spouse, but they have steeled themselves against the work of the Holy Spirit. Their bodies may be in an auditorium, but their hearts and minds are miles away. There is no chance for the Bible to do its work.

Don't be discouraged by those who reject the Bible!

Some Soil is Rocky Soil

In 1 Samuel 16, God sends the mighty prophet Samuel to the family of Jesse telling him that the next king of Israel is there to be anointed. As the oldest son, Eliab, passes by, Samuel is so impressed that he says, "Surely the LORD'S anointed *is* before him." The young man is tall and handsome. He looks like a king.

God has a different point of view. He tells Samuel, "Look not on his countenance, or on the height of his stature; because I have refused him: for *the LORD seeth* not as man seeth; for man lookety on the outward appearance, but the LORD looketh on the heart" (1 Samuel 16:6-7).

Sometimes the seed falls on impressive topsoil. Jesus describes these people as those who "receive the word with joy." Preachers love people who soak up the Word of God with a smile on their face. Every indication tells us that they are real indeed.

But that is only the outward appearance. It is the spiritual topsoil. No human can look into the soul of another, but Jesus knows the rocky ledge lying under the grassy field. The seed cannot take root because the rocks won't allow it, and when the tests and trials of life come, they "fall away." They are never to be found again.

Our look at the outward appearance can be very deceiving. We watch a sinner walk the aisle with tears streaming down his face and are sure that he is the real deal. The stoic who trusts the Lord with no emotion causes us to wonder how real the decision is. This is a big error. Joy is not the distinguishing mark of salvation - obedience is. Jesus said, "If ye continue in my word, *then* are ye my disciples indeed" (John 8:31).

Don't be discouraged by those who fall away!

Some Soil has Thorns

Sometimes, the seed begins to grow. The hearer listens to the Bible and responds to it. Sitting in the church auditorium, the Gospel preaching sounds so attractive. Listening to the soul-winner lay out God's wonderful plan of Salvation sounds too good to be true. When the Gospel is presented, it is such a beautiful thing. How can anyone say no?

All is well until they "go forth." They are not in a church service. They are not in a Bible study. They "go forth" to live their lives, and they learn that the Bible and our culture are incompatible. It seems there is a time element here, and the result is a life that does not bring "fruit to perfection." There may be some fruit, but it never ripens.

Don't be discouraged by those who stop growing!

Some Soil is Good Soil

Whether we are preaching the Gospel from a pulpit, or preaching it across the backyard fence, the sower cannot be swayed by human responses. The faithful sower "shall doubtless come again with rejoicing, bringing his sheaves *with him"* (Psalm 126:6). It is a wonderful day when the seed falls on the good ground.

Good ground is the soil of the "honest and good heart." An honest heart listens to the Bible with no preconceived notions. Instead of selfishly expecting God to do something for them, they want God to show them as they really are. There is no pretense of religion in an honest heart. All of the phony robes of religious hypocrisy are removed. The honest heart comes to Christ 'just as I am.'

The good heart refers to internal qualities. It is the heart of the upright and honorable man. It tells us the man has good character.[11]

The "honest and good heart" belongs to the person who is right on the outside and right on the inside. It is not only an outward expression of faith, but it is also an inward reality. Good soil is produced by this kind of heart. Good soil makes all the effort worthwhile.

It was a stormy night in Birmingham, England, and Hudson Taylor was scheduled to speak in a meeting at the Seven Street Schoolroom. His hostess assured him that nobody would attend on such a stormy night, but Taylor insisted on going. "I must go even if there is no one but the doorkeeper." Less than a dozen people showed up, but the meeting was marked with unusual spiritual power. Half of those present either became missionaries or encouraged their children to be missionaries. The rest were faithful supporters of the work for years to come.[12]

We don't need a big crowd. We don't need great performers. We don't need the latest gadgets. We don't need 'church growth techniques.'

All we need is one *"honest and good heart."*

Chapter Three

THE FIRST TIME Satan speaks in the Old Testament, he says, "Yea, hath God said" (Genesis 3:1). It is an illuminating moment as God exposes Satan's strategy. The devil cannot win unless he destroys the Word of God.

His attack in the Garden of Eden has not changed millennia later. He is still casting doubt on the Bible, misquoting the Bible, and denying the Bible. From the liberal seminary professor who casts aspersions on the Word of God, to the incessant attacks from Satan's forces in high places, the Bible is constantly in his crosshairs.

Sadly, most people have no concern of the onslaught against the Bible. To them, it may be the 'good book,' but it is not worth defending.

It is the same in New Testament times. "Much people" hear Him describe the enemies of the seed, but only his disciples care to ask what it all

27

means. They are the ones who learn the mystery. They discover how Satan attacks the Word of God.

Satan is the Great Enemy

The seed that falls on the hardened wayside does not last very long. The ground does not receive it so it becomes an easy meal for the "fowls of the air." The birds picture the work of Satan on those rare occasions when people actually listen to the Bible. He will not allow the seed to make its way into the heart.

We should notice how quickly Satan works. Luke 8:12 says, "Those by the way side are they that hear; then cometh the devil..." Note the word **"then."** In Mark 4:15, the Bible uses the word "immediately." There is no delay! As soon as the Word is preached, or the moment the witness is given, Satan goes on offense. His biggest nightmare is the sowed Word of God germinating in the human heart. The longer the seed remains, the greater the likelihood that he "should believe and be saved." Satan does not wait.

It is also alarming to note how powerful Satan is. We should never underestimate him! He has the ability to take "away the word out of their hearts." He does not *attempt* to take the word, he actually does so. For him, it as simple as a bird plucking a seed from the wayside. It is a great reminder that a preacher trusting his own flesh, or a soul-winner resting on his own power, is no match for this bird of prey.

How Satan hates the Word the God! His greatest objective is removing the seed from the human heart hardened by our pagan world. He knows the Bible is his enemy.

How Satan must rejoice when Bible preaching is replaced by plays and programs! How tickled he must be to see multitudes of church buildings that once hosted the preaching of the Bible every Sunday night now lying dark and dormant. He must laugh at the ministers who once gathered to preach the Bible, but now they meet to share their ideas. His agenda is to take away the seed at all cost. The very fact that Satan hates the preached Word ought to compel us to preach on!

Satan Uses Times of Temptations

One of the great discouragements of serving the Lord is those who "for a while believe." This is hard to understand and accept. On the surface, things look promising. They "receive the word with joy," but it is a temporary response lasting "for a while." Their superficial religious response to the Bible is exposed by what Jesus refers to as "time of temptation."

The New Testament word not only refers to temptations with reference to lust and sin, but also to any test or examination in the course of life.[13] It would seem that these 'temptations' may be the tests that life often tosses our way. Perhaps an illness, a loss of job, an accident, or another burden puts pressure on the individual. They begin to wonder why God won't fix the problem.

For others, the form of temptation may be a type of persecution. A relative abandons them, a co-worker ridicules them, or a friend leaves them. They discover that a follower of Jesus is required to pay a personal price and it is a cost they won't pay. The Bible says they "fall away." They abandon their relationship with God and forsake Him. "They just quit serving God. They lack root, character, and the grit to endure the Christian life."[14]

Satan Uses Everyday Life

The third soil describes the ones who hear the Bible, but when they "go forth," the "cares and riches and pleasures of *this* life" choke them. These weeds are already in place in the human heart, waiting to do their dirty work.

This list of 'chokers' is stunning. At the top, we are not surprised when Jesus tells us that the "cares" of this world ruin the harvest. Cares are apprehensions, worries, and anxieties. A man full of care frets and panics about tomorrow. Life is full of worry.

However, the next two items listed are unexpected. The "riches and pleasures of *this* life" become spiritual chokers. Our pagan culture takes the opposite approach. We are convinced that "riches" fix the problem of anxiety. A man tells himself, "I have problems. Money will fix my problems. Money will allow me to do what I want with my life." A visit to Disney World will remove all of our troubles.

Money and pleasure! The New Testament word for "pleasures" has given us the English word 'hedonism,' which describes the pursuit of pleasure. It is the byword of our society. People are living for money and fun with the vain hope it will provide relief from worry. Little do they know that these pursuits only choke them all the more. The 'cure' only worsens the disease.

Popular TV ministers who promote the 'prosperity gospel' have a lot to answer for. Joel Osteen wrote: "Every day, we should make positive declarations over our lives. We should say things such as, 'I am blessed. I am prosperous. I am healthy. I am talented. I am creative. I am wise.'"[15] This person could also add, "I am choked."

Gloria Copeland said that she "had been looking at finances and prosperity in a different way from other things, such as divine health … If a symptom of sickness came on my body, I would not stand for it…. You should refuse lack just as quickly as you refuse sickness."[16]

As money piles high in the coffers of false ministers, gullible followers are told they will have their own harvest. They can drive the car they always wanted. They can live in a house they always dreamed of. They will have riches and pleasures. They will never get sick. These 'ministries' should come with a choking hazard warning label.

The consequences of this shallow religion are given by Jesus. They "bring no fruit to perfection." The seed never matures. In some ways, this is more painful than the stony ground or the hard ground. The thorns take a while to choke the plant. It is a slow and gradual process. It is wasted months and years until someone finally admits that they would rather have silver and gold than Jesus.

The faithful sower knows the enemy is great, but he also knows that the Word is greater. Investing in the lives of others can be demoralizing when someone falls away or is choked by the world. But we must keep tossing the seed in the ground. Despite the heartbreaking failures, we have the promise: "...in due season we shall reap, if we faint not" (Galatians 6:9).

Chapter Four

"BUT THAT on the good ground are they, which in an honest and good heart, having heard the word, keep *it*, and bring forth fruit with patience."

This is the reason the sower keeps on sowing the seed. This is the reason the preacher keeps on preaching the Word "in season (and) out of season" (2 Timothy 4:2). This is the reason His servants "go out into the highways and hedges, and compel *them* to come in" (Luke 14:23). We serve Him because we love Him. We want what He wants. The goal is fruit that remains (John 15:16).

The description of the honest and good ground is a beautiful thing to consider.

First, there is a moment in time where a life is changed. "Having heard" brings us back to the hour when we hear the Gospel with our spiritual ears. Every saved person knows that moment. No one grows up into Salvation. No one is gradually saved. There comes that one single point in time when the Spirit of God captures the heart of a sinner, and they respond to the Gospel. It is the second where we pass from "death unto life" (John 5:24). We are "born again" into the family of God (John 3:7). Instantly, we become a "new creature" (2 Corinthians 5:17).

I like the story of the gentleman giving his testimony at a men's meeting. He said, "I went to church with my wife for the longest time. Sunday after Sunday, I listened to the pastor preach the Gospel, but I did not respond. I don't know how many times I left the service unaffected by the preaching. But one Sunday, everything changed. I am not really sure how to say this. I heard, I heard, I heard, but then one day, *I heard*!"

We know what he means.

Secondly, the honest and good ground will "keep" the Word. At first, he may look like the other receivers, but as time progresses, he is different. He does not allow Satan to steal the seed. He does not fall away in time of temptation. He is not going to allow the world to choke him. He not only keeps it, but he also 'keeps on' keeping it.[17] In other verses in the New Testament, we read the word as "holding fast."[18] No one can pry the Bible out of his life!

Next, the Bible says the good ground will "bring forth fruit." With some, such a statement is controversial, but the point is clear in the Bible. Saved people produce spiritual fruit. "For we are his workmanship, created in Christ Jesus unto good works, which God hath before ordained that we should walk in them" (Ephesians 2:10). "But the fruit of the Spirit is love, joy, peace, longsuffering, gentleness, goodness, faith, meekness, temperance: against such there is no law" (Galatians 5:22-23). There are no examples of people in the Bible who are saved but do not produce fruit.

Finally, the good ground will "bring forth fruit with patience." This marks the difference between the soils. When the pressures of the world mount, the good ground "bears up under difficult circumstances."[19] The child of God abides in Christ.

One of the saddest pictures in the Bible is found in 1 John 2:19. Old Pastor John has spent a lifetime preaching the Gospel of his Lord and investing his life in people. But now, a brokenhearted man of God thinks of those who have abandoned the Lord. "They went out from us, but they were not of us; for if they had been of us, they would *no doubt* have continued with us: but *they went out*, that they might be made manifest that they were not all of us."

"They would *no doubt* have continued with us." Perhaps some of the people we call 'backsliders' are really people who "were not of us."

This is truly the confusing point of the entire parable: which of these soils illustrate those who are saved, and which of the soils illustrate those who are lost? Through the centuries, preachers have debated the argument. Obviously, the good ground describes one who is saved without a doubt. But what about the other three cases?

Is the man saved who hears the word and then Satan comes immediately and takes it away? It would seem to me that this illustrates a man that is not saved, but not all see it that way.[20] What about those who "for a while believe?" What about the person who has some fruit, but not "to perfection?" The debates are endless.

Perhaps that is the point of the parable. Jesus never stopped and said, "This guy is saved. This guy is not saved." Maybe the big picture tells us that salvation is so critical, we had better "give diligence to make (our) calling and election sure" (2 Peter 1:10). There are times when we need to put the brakes on our busy lives and heed 2 Corinthians 13:5: "Examine yourselves, whether ye be in the faith; prove your own selves. Know ye not your own selves, how that Jesus Christ is in you, except ye be reprobates?"

There is no doubt about the man who has an honest and good heart! There is no doubt about the man who hears the Word of God and keeps it! There is no doubt about the man who brings forth fruit with patience!

No doubt! That is the Christian life I want. There is no doubt about someone who craves and desires the Bible every day. There is no doubt about someone who is producing Bible results in his daily walk. There is no doubt about someone who spends a lifetime loving God's Word.

We need to determine that we will never allow ourselves to get cold towards our Bible. We need to prioritize the Bible in our daily schedules.

In the late 1800's, a young music teacher, Palmer Hartsough, was faithfully serving the Lord in his church. For decades he used his talents in music to write hymns that exalted Christ. At the age of sixty-two, God called him to preach. A few years later, God led him to a Baptist church in Ontario, Michigan, where he pastored for a number of years.

Pastor Hartsough's life was a testimony to faithfulness. Whether a serving member of a local church, or a pastor leading a flock, he followed the Will of God and the Word of God with a consistency that lasted for decades. He knew the secret, and gave it to us in these words:

I am resolved, and who will go with me?
Come, friends, without delay;
Taught by the Bible, led by the Spirit,
We'll walk the heav'nly way.[21]

A wise person once said, "The Bible will keep me from sin, and sin will keep me from the Bible." Perhaps we might add these words to that sage advice:

> *The Bible will keep me from doubt,*
> *and doubt will keep me from the Bible.*

Chapter Five

IT IS THE WORK God's people are called to perform. We already know that some seeds will not bring forth fruit, but other seeds will reproduce beyond our wildest imagination. It is not the skill of the sower that produces the harvest. There is nothing particularly difficult about reaching into a bag and tossing seed on the ground. Rather, it is the faithfulness of the sower that God blesses.

The sower cannot tell what the ground is like. If we knew where the best soil existed, we might avoid places where God intends to do a work. God's harvests do not have to be large to be effective. One seed in one heart may be the only result of years of effort, but we do not despise the "day of small things" (Zechariah 4:10). It is God's seed. It is God's harvest.

God told the prophet Ezekiel, "Whether they will hear, or whether they will forbear ... yet shall know that there hath been a prophet among them" (Ezekiel 2:5). Regardless of the response of the world, our mission is still the same. From the pulpit to the backyard fence, the sower is called upon to disseminate the perfect seed. The unsaved man does not need him to be funny, cute, imaginative, or entertaining. The lost man needs a sower who is faithful.

In 1780, the noonday skies over the city of Hartford, Connecticut, turned from blue to gray. By mid-afternoon, the city had darkened over so densely that, in that religious age, men fell on their knees and begged a final blessing before the end of the world descended. The Connecticut House of Delegates was in session. There was pandemonium, and many members of the House were calling for adjournment.

The Speaker of the House, Colonel Abraham Davenport, rose to his feet, and silenced the din with these famous words:

"The Day of Judgment is either at hand or it is not at hand. If it is not, there is no need for adjournment. If it is, I choose to be found by my God doing my duty. I entertain the motion,

therefore, that candles be brought to enlighten this hall of democracy."[22]

The day is coming when the "the Lord himself shall descend from heaven with a shout, with the voice of the archangel, and with the trump of God" (1 Thessalonians 4:16). When that moment comes, should we be the generation to meet Him in the air, may He find us actively doing the Master's business.

> *"And let us not be weary in well doing:*
> *for in due season we shall reap,*
> *if we faint not."*

Endnotes

1. Luke 4:14-15; 4:37; 4:42; 5:1; 5:15; 5:19; 5:29; 6:17-19; 7:11.

2. https://ministrytodaymag.com/leadership/counseling/20036-rick-warren-8-steps-to-grow-your-church

3. Bock, D. L. (1994). *Luke: 1:1–9:50* (Vol. 1, pp. 723–724). Grand Rapids, MI: Baker Academic.

4. Edwards, J. R. (2015). *The Gospel according to Luke*. (D. A. Carson, Ed.) (pp. 235–236). Grand Rapids, MI; Cambridge, U.K.; Nottingham, England: William B. Eerdmans Publishing Company; Apollos.

5. Bock, D. L. (1994). *Luke: 1:1–9:50* (Vol. 1, p. 724). Grand Rapids, MI: Baker Academic.

6. Bock, D. L. (1994). *Luke: 1:1–9:50* (Vol. 1, p. 725). Grand Rapids, MI: Baker Academic.

7. Tan, P. L. (1996). *Encyclopedia of 7700 Illustrations: Signs of the Times* (p. 1328). Garland, TX: Bible Communications, Inc.

8. Matthew 11:15; Matthew 13:9; Matthew 13:43; Mark 4:12; Mark 7:16; Luke 8:8; Luke 14:35.

9. Revelation 2:7; 2:11; 2:17; 2:29; 3:6; 3:13; 3:22; 13:9.

10. Phillips, John (2005). *Exploring the Gospel of Luke: An Expository Commentary*. Grand Rapids, MI: Kregel Academics.

11. Sorenson, D. H. (2007). *Understanding the Bible, An Independent Baptist Commentary Matthew through Luke* (Vol. 8, p. 641). Northstar.

12. Galaxie Software. (2002). *10,000 Sermon Illustrations*. Biblical Studies Press.

13. Zodhiates, S. (2000). *The complete word study dictionary: New Testament* (electronic ed.). Chattanooga, TN: AMG Publishers.

14. Sorenson, D. H. (2007). *Understanding the Bible, An Independent Baptist Commentary Matthew through Luke* (Vol. 8, p. 640). Northstar.

15. Bowler, Kate. Blessed: A History of the American Prosperity Gospel (Kindle Locations 2282-2284). Oxford University Press. Kindle Edition.

16. Ibid.

17. The language of the New Testament uses a present active verb. This indicates an action that begins and does not stop.

18. 1 Thessalonians 5:21; Hebrews 10:23

19. Louw, J. P., & Nida, E. A. (1996). *Greek-English lexicon of the New Testament: based on semantic domains* (electronic ed. of the 2nd edition., Vol. 1, p. 307). New York: United Bible Societies.

20. Bock, D. L. (1994). *Luke: 1:1–9:50* (Vol. 1, pp. 733–734). Grand Rapids, MI: Baker Academic. (Note that the author does not hold his position; he refers to others who would claim that all four soils represent saved people.)

21. https://hymnstudiesblog.wordpress.com/2008/06/28/quoti-am-resolvedquot/

22. Morgan, R. J. (2000). *Nelson's complete book of stories, illustrations, and quotes* (electronic ed., p. 503). Nashville: Thomas Nelson Publishers.

*"For the preaching of the cross
is to them that perish foolishness;
but unto us which are saved
it is the power of God."*
(1 Corinthians 1:18)

You are invited to hear Evangelist
Paul Schwanke. His schedule of
meetings can be found here:

www.preachthebible.com

Made in the USA
Middletown, DE
30 September 2023

39612744R00033